After the Rain

After the Rain

Jonathan A. Wright

Gallery of Readers Press
Northampton, Massachusetts
2014

Text copyright ©2014 Jonathan A. Wright.
All rights reserved.
Author photograph by Amy Elizabeth Wright.
Cover image ©2014 Page Allen.
Photographed by James Hart, Santa Fe, NM. Courtesy of The
Owings Gallery, Santa Fe, NM.

This book was designed and typeset by Stephanie Gibbs; printed
and bound at Bridgeport National Bindery, Agawam, MA.

Gallery of Readers Press
Carol Edelstein & Robin Barber, Editors
16 Vernon Street
Northampton, Massachusetts 01060
www.galleryofreaders.org

ISBN 978-0-9829448-8-2

For Meg:

> Thank you for believing
> For reading, holding, loving, laughing
> For everything and always

Table of Contents

1

2

Hexagram

4

5

1

By Morning

Rain pounded the flashings
and the meadow all night;
now, the impossibly green
tall grass by the pond weaves
its tapestry of wind-rustle and morning.

A slight ripple in the mocha water
hints at fish,
luminous gold and silver carp,
catfish with their awful whiskers
gliding through the murk.

A story comes to be
without anything
ever happening
except a summer rain.

After the Rain

The tide went out
after the rain, after dawn,
taking the river with it,
tangles of rope and fish line,
shreds of children's clothes,
and rubber shoe soles,
grounding, wrecking, beaching
bamboo root clumps
the size of dump trucks
into the ocean sand,
fresh, cunning, wild
shoots sprayed out.

Bearded coconut heads
loll in the slackened wash,
a massacre of vegetation,
sleek with silt and promise,
unarmed and fleeing,
feeding dogfish and pearls.
I would not miss
what comes of this so quick,
so soon after the rain.

Our still wet skin
glistens and reminds me
not long ago we were yet unborn,
content, kicking in brine,
and long, long before and so small,

came from water,
slippery, still mostly liquid,
sparkling like flint or rain,
with tails and short legs,
for the very first time,
into the sun.

Old Grief

Don't work so hard
to keep the grief alive;
it knows how
to live quite well
in my body on its own,
sweeping birthday surprises
and night sadness sweats
into soiled mesh bags of longing.

Unfold them, handle them,
your paint-spattered,
putty-crusted dirt brocades.
Hang them on a line of cares
between two apple trees and think
of them as saffron Tibetan prayers.
Quiet-mind the tatters and the tears.
Strip the grieving body skin.
Release the lather, cries and laughter,
the muscle burn of
love-commanded heat
burst out within.

Getting Started

The castle dreamt itself to rubble;
its stones and quicklime slowly
washed into the creek and bight;
the sword lies wrapped in oiled cloth.
A pen, mighty and still, is in its jar
next to where the door once was,
looking out over an ink-blue sea.

The sand is white and hot like paper;
the paper, smooth as skin.
The skin, with its flesh akin
to rubber and wind and smoke,
is where I end and you begin,
and where the day made
of all these things,
abraded, washed, polished,
awakes.

Rowing in Shad Season

She's hurled her love-mad way upstream.
After tidal surfing in estuaries,
slipping over sandbars,
weedy rocks and concrete ladders,
weeks of plunging headlong,
blind, driven by destiny she drops
thirty thousand eggs in her
sex-life debut and farewell
under the watchful eyes
of osprey, hawk and heron.

Finished now, fury gone,
she rolls slowly onto her side,
her up-eye filmed with dawn sky,
her dorsal slack. Her puckered
seersucker pajama–skin cheek
catches my glance. Eye to eye
we meet in the river,
wet, cold and spent, wondering
what will become of us.

Gravel, Truck, Bagpiper

Tire and diesel whine
along the far shore;
up close, gravel,
like rain-stick beads,
slides down the steel
truck bed.

The bagpiper's rising wind
drifts across the lowland fields,
a mourning toward midday;
a sadness so certain,
I am comforted.

Short Story

Lifted by sorrow,
felled by purpose,
soothed by longing,
loved by air,
shaped by stone,
rusted by stars,
seeded by wind,
washed by dirt,
burned by blindness,
scalded by work,
weighed by dark,
pounded by needles,
ended by dawn.

Breakers

With a sweat dark leather
bronze hand heel thimble
sail maker's palm,
sanded mammal bone needle,
and Irish bees' waxed flaxen thread,
driftwood weathered fingers
stitch a rough sea foam
dimpled skirt of surf
on the sleek bare
body of water.

Mount Hope Bay

The water is clear
on the incoming tide,
rippled like auburn silk;
three geese, two ducks
and a single plover pass,
as the last sunlight bursts
on weathered pilings,
on heather,
on late climbing roses and bittersweet,
on honeysuckle and heron beaks,
on rosa rugosa stems and thorn fur,
and sprays a last blazing
wild lovestruck
water-prismed glow.

My Pond

has three kinds of frogs,
voices mud-sunk low and wet by day,
livened in the failing snipe-mating
twilight into a handsome trio.
The donkey frog brays deep
and lonesome for his barnyard beloved.
The bass Jews' harp frog,
no tenor or lieder, just a twangy thud.
Above, the yodel frog
calls the nymphs and sheriffs out
to dance the water down
and fireflies about.
You might think the world asleep
but the conclave of dirt,
sludge and mire sex
has just begun.

Nothing, Something, Everything

Nothing is so still as when
night shrugs up a day
and the wind's all down;
the wren stops by the barn ridge
to catch a darting glimpse
of where the dawn went
atop West Hill.

Something of the last few flakes of snow
seems more about a lesson still unlearned,
and right at hand, not yet known,
than the winter's wooden fingers
unclasping now and letting go.

Everything gives up its linger, gone away,
lungs hollowed out by air,
bound by bendy thought and bones so spare.
The mind is all drained away
of solids and the pigments too,
even stories are settled down to still.
The heart is given in to other magic things,
driven out of dawn:
first and brilliant light
breaking there.

2

Two Lives

Unlike cats with their nine lives
or Christians born again and again
in wild Midwestern summer tents,
I have only two lives:
the one that's given,
wrapped in cotton tatters
and the silk of mother-skin,
the slender woven arms
of fever-softened love;
and the one that's taken away,
bound but not burned or buried
or mistaken for the rush of water.

Which one is it now that rustles up
the winter-withered linden leaves
and comes, crouching in the dark of damp
late winter, hands and bony limbs
cold-stiffened, its blood pooling
at the edge of dawn,
calling for our tiny carp
and salamander hearts
to swim again
before we go?

Instructions

Dry my face with sparrow wings,
comb my hair by oil lamp.
Spice the barren limbs
with lavender and salt.
Stop the sun with a finger;
start the river with a smile.
Reach across with a hush.
Kiss again with a naked sky.

Just this little bit
might raise the moon
and light the night,
make sorrow
into cookie crumbs,
and boundless dread
into a Celtic tune
a child could tap out
on his cocoa cup
with a spoon.

Origin

Do you know where
you came from,
who first, the very, very
first, called your name?
As for me, I came upon
an answer on tiptoe
in soft wet grass,
in the way that night
falls slowly
in midsummer.

An earthworm, ruddy,
wet, spaded in two,
wiggled out from under
the apple tree roots
on the day the blossoms
flew away.

River Morning

Near-black water,
wrinkled like old cotton,
wind brushed
like suede leather;
tree shroud of empty-handed
wind-fist, leaves upturned,
looks east, rain coming
fast now,
at the last stillness.

Woodpecker, Wind, Raven

Cloud bent light
spills down the meadow,
fills in below the willows
and the linden stand;
morning calm clipped
into heartbeat bits
by more than one
woodpecker, breakfasting.

The wind is not the wind
but this water's creek and tumble
calling back, conifer night sound
mistaken now for breathing.

As for the raven,
I brought it here myself
in a softened
hand of centuries,
in the way of the Inuit,
the Hopi, or the Tlingit;
a clannish sense
of being, for a moment,
always and everywhere
at once.

Dark Harmony

Wet bark on bare trees
on the river bank
casts its umber glow
on the black twilit water.
The trunks are
wound with bittersweet
and berries tinting
the afternoon and water
softly red.

Nothing moves but the darkness
falling toward night,
the river falling
toward ocean,
these old trees falling
toward their perfect
reflection in the river,
while an ancient stillness
rises through me
in their path.

In the Shade

Breaking waves sound like
something beaten, hammered,
doused and forged;
industry, percussion, touch:
"listen, cry out, hiss, forgive,"
they say in English.
"Kiss, drift, die out, breathe again,"
in local dialect; all day
the northeast trades fill in.

In a single glance I see
a gleam on her brown shoulder
just below the red halter strap
where his tongue has coursed,
her hair pulled back
falling like rain onto his neck;
she sits on his left thigh,
back pressed
into his chest,
legs braided together
like shipping hawsers,
and eyes gleaming
like the ocean would,
if it were chocolate,
melting slowly
onto sea grape leaves.

Your New Love

I have long befriended
from a gentle distance
the silky black busy bird
inhabiting your face,
the glistening Aegean coast
starlit night of your body,
where, today, a soft mammal
with eyes like kalamata olives,
skin of fresh-caught white bream
has taken up residence, cuddled
into your freshened cheeks,
beached its weathered dory
and stowed its weary paddle,
licking the high noon
tide pools of your
new love smile.

Though not for me,
this smile,
who could not,
touched on the neck or
wrist or chin,
turn toward the hot,
damp south wind
of it?

If

If we could have been cats,
I would have licked and preened
your soft blond fur all over,
with no care at all
for a hairball,
under a night quilt,
hidden by candles and breath.
We might still be laughing
after we could
no longer stand
the heat and wet.

But I was too shy
and still burning
with a smoky sorrow
to smile and touch you.
I looked away instead.
It's in the book I didn't write,
you never read.
The purring now
comes as late peepers or
a farmer's diesel
river pump, in my head.

I remember you
as spring water drops
dancing on the hot
smooth wax of summer.

Loiza Beach

Walking west toward the river inlet,
at first I saw rubbish and sticks
and something like tissues
in the sand;
party remnants maybe,
washed in or washed out.

Up close I saw
dozens of oranges and apples
polished by water and sand,
not a bite or blemish anywhere.
The paper things, why, they are
scores of freshly wilted roses,
white as noon.
No other signs of funeral
or wedding traffic, baptismal rites,
footprints or tire tracks;
just petals and stems,
slowly parting.

Returning back this way
an hour later and the tide falling
the beach is empty, clean now
except for two apples, one orange,
and suddenly a watermelon
rolling in the wash,
its weeks-dead flesh still fresh,
perhaps lightly salted
for my half-southern tongue.

Just here yesterday
a drained and drowned,
livid green iguana lay,
nothing gone from him but life;
after one misjudged breaker,
he's left his party dress,
a slackened, striped, and silky rind.

The roses made their point,
came and went
at the white edge of the sea,
toasted and curled by sand.

And the tender, gleaming fruits —
what sort of longing is it
with which I miss them now?

Dusk Comes to the Old Pirate

Surf pounds on the bar like a train
that never arrives,
a surge and ebb in the valleys of sea;
the air is as sweet as a peach and salty as nuts.
He thinks of his cigar and holds
a tube of bamboo; touching his right shoulder
where his gray parrot Distant Thunder once sat,
he finds a ragged shirtsleeve
smelling of nutmeg, lime and gunpowder.
In his other hand, rusty keys
have replaced the dagger.
His gold earring remains.
Turning, he steps toward the wash,
thinking it is time to launch the captain's gig.
Finding none, he gazes at the dusk-horizon
for clues of foundered ships.
Tonight and every night now there is only
the final dancing blaze of the bright red
Magic Lantern under full and glowing canvas
going down in the western sea.

Outbound

Gale force winds are forecast
off the Isle of Shoals,
the shallows of beckon,
of waves breaking and treachery.
Hear the gusts rise
in the schooner's rigging,
the moan of devil and dark,
the ship's lee rail is down;
phosphorescence bubbles
in the scuppers of black night;
a single gimbaled cabin light
brightens for you, the captain
of the *Failing Forward*;
you lift and settle your pen
in the logbook like
there is no tomorrow.

Waiting

Shallow and rapid now, where the water is thin
and the bottom grass sways downstream;
her breathing, short, quick,
tumbles over the stones.
Within hours now
she'll run dry
like a summer creek,
done with ice chips and swabs,
and the wide shallows of bedside,
and slip away —
eyes closed, feet cool,
fresh current-driven,
on a fair tide
to the other side.

Sunset

with thanks to Tu Fu (712–770 A.D.)

Sunlight shatters
on the curtain beads.
Spring flowers scatter
into the valley.
Gardens along the river
are listless with perfume.
Smoke of cook fires
boils over the slow barges.
Sparrows shriek and fall in the branches.
Whirling insects die in midair.
Who could believe
that one cup of thick wine
will enflame a thousand cares?

Hexagram

No Vacancy

What could this mean
in neon above the sign
for Nine Pines Motel?
Two cars parked out back,
a dirt track vanishes
into the woods.

Yellow lightbulbs burn
outside each
of eight queen
bed rooms.
I smell pine sap, burnt toast
and something like
late snow coming.

What is left to be empty?
Where do the two
cars go when the "No"
goes unlit?

Vacancy

Emptiness is everywhere;
even physicists agree
with medicine men
and television evangelists
that there is, in this
vast space between
atoms and particles,
the total emptiness
between Providence and Boston,
a little electricity
of attraction
or abhorrence, the desire
not to touch, or touch.
Not just nothing,
as long supposed,
but openness through which
light passes unopposed.

Open Window

Water pools on the sill,
a breeze drifts over me:
a tuft of fresh cotton.
Cool steady rain
rises at night to a torrent,
then abates to drizzle,
invisible in the dark.
Wrapped in textile undergrowth,
my bedcovers are lichen,
sticks and moss;
we mammals tiptoe
in and out of dreams,
the glassy shine of morning
still hours away.

Fabric

The prop-jet cruises
just above the cloud
wrung of its water,
light as a pillow.
Nothing known
beyond police notes,
wet roads, head-on crash,
and all that's left now broken,
in a wooden box.
How this happened is an answer
begging the question.
Soggy handkerchief
still in my pocket.

Box

What's left of the body
is still too heavy even
after the smoke dies.
Ash and bone chips weigh
more than we can bear
down to the edge
of the lake.

Lake Superior

Clear as sky, almost vacant,
deep bending light folds
around the bottom stones;
a sudden ripple
shaking like your puppy
nibbles on the dark
soft rim of shore.
You are here with us,
where the bottom
drops quickly away.

Superior is a place apart,
more ocean than lake,
more ancient than known,
and cold enough any day
to burn right through;
there is no place like this
without you.

4

End of March

Befriend the rake, the rising wind,
whose winter face is leathered, kindness gone.
Twigs shake off their mold of soil and frost.
Leaves toss and dream, crumbled,
shattered, lost.
The trail to spring
is heaved with murmur,
then roars with a warming quest:
lean in, pull and press,
the clouds never rest.

Calendula

Spring flood abated and
silted woods floor
sprung with fiddleheads, ripples of light,
and yellow-blossomed calendula,
an almanac of undulated days
between planting moons;
calendula, the salve for babies
in their first spring,
the restless bark and bakery
of cinnamon and turbinado;
calendula, early flower, flourishing like
cold creek salmon fry
before the maples leaf;
calendula, flickering candle
with endless cotton wicks;
calendula, the pendulum of Scotland
swings in Caledonia;
calendula, between breaths
you rest on the tip of the edge
of the river of my tongue,
then are swallowed, thirsty, dark,
dredged with petals and duff
into summer.

Plums

Words, like plums,
should be soft on the tongue,
leaving a trace of something like
warm sunlit stones in the throat,
turning to lemon, honey
and water at dusk.

Fresh wine and bitter greens
create a longing for
potatoes and olives,
easily mistaken
for a love close by
which thrives
on a steady diet
of ripe plums.

Grief Again

Grief tonight shakes you weightless;
the wind could break away
and bear you high aloft.
Come back, please come back
from the daily wrack
of your mother's
final flight.

Wrap it around me
like a blackened sash
and I'll walk it out
into another life
from which I promise
I will return for you
on wings another night.

Impossible

Summer deep sky;
copper beech leaves
dance to windward;
the blue braided clothesline,
with its blue plastic pins and clips,
dips and sags;
something sky-blue
flickers on the fence post cap:
copper fleck and dusted wing cape
make this eastern bluebird
impossible and true.

Another World

You might be as surprised as I was,
that the edge of another world,
seven feet due west
of my hospital bed,
was filled with a warm
summer breeze.

The curtains billowed in
the open windows;
hyacinths and chrysanthemums
were all about the foyer,
while the radiant afternoon
collected at the foot of the bed
where you thought you stood
in a white and windowless room.

French doors opened
onto a shaded porch
with geranium pots and courting swings;
birds sang without stopping
and everywhere the murmur
of family like falling water.

I will sit on that porch one day,
not just now, I think, or so the doctors said.
I will smell the ripening pears,
admire yellow, white and crimson roses,
the orange pyracantha berries,
feel the steady breeze
off an ocean I cannot see.

I will hold your hand again,
and you, whom I have held close
with eyes closed,
will tell me your real name.

Upon Hearing a Texas Poet

Your voice rose soft and early
for cold grits and butter,
slipped through the piney woods mist
down the red clay
mud swallow-nested river bank,
forded the slough with nothing but
green back scales showing,
shed its skin
but not its love of kin,
then ginned tall tales and cotton,
picking green lima beans before dancing 'til dawn
at Chez Pauline's in Baton Rouge.

Cornbread and gravy gave way
to night-skipping through Jackson,
where your footfalls were heard
like the crunch of young teeth
on pralines before
a sip of buttermilk,
coming to rest
wrapped in corn silk
and an owl's whisper,
like Woodie Guthrie's baby sister,
in my sleeping Tuscaloosa heart,
where your voice
awoke a longing, for watermelon,
greens and crab,
but not bourbon and pot liquor,

set the stars to falling over Alabama
and the moon to rise on your call,
right at home, such a long,
long way from West Texas.

We Had a Mother Once

Certain days, when forgetting
unties itself of truss
and twine and bony
simple supple grief,
there you are.
I wish you'd say just a word or two
while passing by.

You read us quite a few
whole books
twice aloud, all through.
Just the name of David Copperfield,
spoken now, would do.
The gone years since are forty-two
and some, but who is tracking
the numbers now?

Most of those you knew
are dead or going, counting slowly,
drawn by the smell of fruit,
and God and fear.
It's your face and hands, and the hot silly love
for little boys with close-cut hair and antics
that drove you happy happy crazy,
that I miss most.

Only one brother and I are left
who know what you could do,
even pushed, crushed, scoured of brain,
sorrow and heart, punished hard

for growing dreams of a life breaking free,
by booze and pills and the sorry lot of softened men.

No one before broke through like you
made so what never was before,
you the better, no, the very best,
even shattered and abed
with a murder mystery,
buttermilk, saltines.
There was no glory offered you, once spent;
cancer came where depression went.
A peaceful time of smiles ushered in
a withering of mind and bones and skin.

All I've ever done is learn
by hard and softly crying
to promise kindness can be born
again of rage, of ancient sweetness
cast aside, reclaimed.
That's how fresh and
hardy tubers, storms,
and families are made.

Dead River Row

For miles the Dead River's banks
are barely a rise of cypress roots
like giant bundled cinnamon sticks
hugging more knees,
and traces of roots,
and bark and leaves
wrapped around eight thousand years
of apple snail–shell midden.
"Ha. Ha. Ha. Ha …" calls the pied-billed grebe.

Who can forget
the Spanish Christian rape,
cataloged in detail by monk and priest,
of the Timucua river people:
though vanished now we can see
their three souls —
one in the pupil of the eye,
another in our cast shadow,
and a third, our reflection
in clear black water?

Three parasitic air plants
have latched onto a sable palm:
Spanish moss, resurrection fern —
green for one day after rain —
and a wild orchid blossom
the size of a peppercorn.

"Ark. Ark. Ark …" the great blue heron
calls three times,
Morse code from the Pleistocene
from one who cannot swim,
barely sings.

The anhinga dries her black
oil-free wings, holding her head high
on snakelike neck,
while the secretive limpkins
call among themselves without distress
"ahhhrrrrr,"
and tiptoe through the brush
like yard chickens.

Along the Dead River
a fine silt of peace fills in
the creeks and sloughs;
all three souls awash
in the gray sparkle
of rain on my skin;
how strokes on the oar
grow stronger
as words hush down.

Listen quietly
for what is not me:

threes upon threes upon threes
wrap around my roots,
my knees, my would-be wings.

Every leaf and whole
or broken tree,
listening, breathing still,
is wood and flower
and bird, and sings.

Learning Curve

I learned, I think it was
the hard way, to love you,
at the bedside of "it's better
not to," at the unscheduled
Monday morning curbside
pickup of go to hell,
in the kitchen of hazy, hot,
and humid, in the winter
of hurting deeply, followed
by the spring of badly folding
laundry, standing in
the "order here" line for
takeout family life.
I was sipping forgetfulness
with ice and a twist and still
you tiptoed up the stairs
into my dream and boiling house
to hear "I'm tired, I'm sorry"
and still, because at least,
like a small black dog, I am loyal
with the only sticks I can find
and fetch, I tried to find you.
On your night watch
you found the story
in which you forgave me,
and read it aloud
as if it were the news,
and it is. It's true.

Questions

What will become of me,
my soft rain-dropped
love for you, hanging low
like fresh laundry,
a setting day-rinsed sun
in its indigo night collar,
in that linden tree?

How long have I been
watching your night-cool
bare arm on the pillow
by my head,
waiting for first light
or your slight movement
to excuse a slow brush
along the soft kitten
of your skin
sleeping there?

5

Evening Hill

You can see among the winter
toasted oak and linden sticks
the feathered limey
bottle brushed and stark
naked maples stripped
for the river freshet,
and the footbridge
last week heaved about.
The trees have shed
their reddened tips
like scalded lips and hurry
restless into broad-lit night.

Gust

Sweat-lathered in pollen
and small mammal scent
it bursts in the open window,
scattering papers, sweeping
dog hair and dust,
abandoned cornflakes,
dry threads, across
the glistening bright red
fender of morning.

Trailing its white
Buddhist gift shawl
across the clatter of dress shoes,
garden clogs, glass slippers and
the leaf moccasins of ancient
druids, it crosses to
the other window,
breathing softly now,
hesitates, trembling
against the insect screen
before passing through.

Hot Out

From the car I got
just a glimpse of a shirtless man,
after the day's heat had peaked
and early evening offered shade,
walking up from the creek with his girlfriend,
his leg tattoos showing
below the cutoff Army pants,
long hair still wet, and in the crook of his arm,
a sleeping baby,
still river-gleaming and so quiet
she could have been
part of him, was part of him,
save what gave her away,
her burrowed head, and the pudgy folds
of her soft arm against
the sandy wisps of hair
on his bony chest just below
where the dragonfly pendant
hung from its leather lanyard.

Work

Down to the blue wire.
Words cry softly in the dark.
Night work never ends.

Last Scull

The river is so low
in the wide straight stretch,
a white egret strolls
bank to bank
over gravel shoals
like northern sea flats
at ebb tide.

What's left for us is
more sky than water;
we follow hidden channels
where the bottom comes up slow
and rubble-stoned to meet us.

Streams cut sand the way
wind carves clouds
and we row one last
time in a wet
sweet unknown
between.

Born Again

Before first light, a wolf howls
three times in his thinly frosted
beech and oak and bramble church.
Downhill, one apple and two
white-stubble-whiskered
birch trees
guard the last mowing.

All the trees have
cleaned themselves like cats,
licking away the last leaves with
smoke-sweetened wind tongues,
leaving their love-bones to dry,
freeze, and be born again,
as I am now, straightening
some twisted turns of phrase
into long, wet, supple
apple limbs worth
climbing in.

Total Recall

When the freshly minted
mountainside of day awakes
with hints of lavender and birch
bent and curled from winter,
stumps sprouting long and wintered,
I want to take your hand,
ungloved, inside the failing wind,
where you gather new rain
and lift the unseen
into full view.

The hillside is a muscled,
tendoned, weathered mammal's back,
rubbled and spent from looking hard for true —
clouds go slack and soft and nearly blue;
remind me of what is newly lost of me:
it remains in water, fiber, air and bark —
and bird and you.

Estuary

At the bend by the highway bridge,
slow water and bamboo give way
to the open river, a stucco chapel
on one side, shuttered, rust-streaked;
on the other, a long-abandoned sugar mill.

High banks with mud swallows' nests
give way to open grassland,
tamarinds, blue heron, and white ibis,
kingfisher and osprey with their creaky
swinging screen-door cries.
Flood trash shopping bags
hang from upper limbs;
above eddies of mountain-grass shreds,
flip-flops and weathered hat brims.
A shearwater skims, deep inshore,
where the fickle breeze
gives way to steady wind.
Tawny water gives way
to gray, to green,
to sudden salted blue.
Coconuts, oranges, one perished pig
drift slowly by.

Here the floodwaters spread out
toward an old racehorse
grazing by a fishing shanty,
roof caved in,
long ago given way
to mangrove thicket

in brooding black water.
Plovers, swallows, doves
and hummingbirds give way
to pelicans and a frigate bird,
with its delta wing,
coasting high, still,
into the wind.

Surf calls, pounds its white
cloud ribbon lip and churns
the horizon, flips it up,
lathers it with trade wind
and spindrift,
then swallows it whole
where the sky tumbles in,
gives way to the sea.

Getting Late

The afternoon is a lake where at last
I can see myself in the shallows
where the cedar roots run clear.
Maples are bare and near, as I read
about Buddha and the twelve steps,
their trunks turn tawny, copper,
tarnished bronze with a touch of umber;
where secrets keep,
clouds hint of thunder, awaken;
light fails faster, brightening.

Acknowledgments

To Carol Edelstein and Robin Barber of Gallery of Readers Press, for the shelter of love and confidence, for inviting my voice into this new and freshened life.

To Francis Smith, John Stifler, John Boettiger, Michael Benedikt, Christopher Lydon, the late Heather McClave, and the late and beloved David Smith, for your encouragement, faith and loyalty over five decades.

To Mary Clabaugh Wright and Arthur F. Wright, my parents, who started this adventure of mine, and who, though long deceased, still provide their companionship of genes, voice, and mystery.

To the bright, funny, lovable Wednesday Night writers: without you, many of these pages would be listless or blank.

To my thoughtful readers: Meg Kelsey Wright, Russell Powell, the Rt. Reverend Rob Hirschfeld, Christopher Lydon, Chase Twichell, for your abundance of time and insights.

To Page Allen especially, for more than forty years of stunning artwork, books and friendship, and for the cover art for this book, which makes it whole.

To the underwriters of Gallery of Readers Press: Thank you!

To Stephanie Gibbs, whose eye and ear and hand are coursed with genius, for the book design, and to Norma

Sims Roche, whose editorial eye can exact intended meaning from mere suggestion.

To my friends and co-workers at Wright Builders who have helped me make time to write.

To my wife Meg, to Anna, Nick, Amy and Andrew; to my brother Duncan and dear cousins, for support, faith, interest and companionship on this path.

About the Author

Jonathan A. Wright has been developing his writing skills since childhood. In 1974, he was part of Hampshire College's first graduating class. Over the past forty years, he has created and managed two construction industry companies. Wright Architectural Millwork Inc. is now thriving in the capable hands of two former colleagues. Wright Builders Inc., of which Jonathan is co-principal, has pioneered energy-efficient construction and a collaborative design approach, and is a leader in sustainable design and construction in western New England. Jonathan is known as an avid sculler and coach, as well as for his many contributions to the arts, education and health of the Northampton, Massachusetts, community where he lives with his wife Meg. They have three grown children and one grandson.